Reform of the International Monetary Fund

Peter B. Kenen

CSR NO. 29, MAY 2007
COUNCIL ON FOREIGN RELATIONS

Founded in 1921, the Council on Foreign Relations is an independent, national membership organization and a nonpartisan center for scholars dedicated to producing and disseminating ideas so that individual and corporate members, as well as policymakers, journalists, students, and interested citizens in the United States and other countries, can better understand the world and the foreign policy choices facing the United States and other governments. The Council does this by convening meetings; conducting a wide-ranging Studies Program; publishing *Foreign Affairs*, the preeminent journal covering international affairs and U.S. foreign policy; maintaining a diverse membership; sponsoring Independent Task Forces and Special Reports; and providing up-to-date information about the world and U.S. foreign policy on the Council's website, CFR.org.

THE COUNCIL TAKES NO INSTITUTIONAL POSITION ON POLICY ISSUES AND HAS NO AFFILIATION WITH THE U.S. GOVERNMENT. ALL STATEMENTS OF FACT AND EXPRESSIONS OF OPINION CONTAINED IN ITS PUBLICATIONS ARE THE SOLE RESPONSIBILITY OF THE AUTHOR OR AUTHORS.

Council Special Reports (CSRs) are concise policy briefs, produced to provide a rapid response to a developing crisis or contribute to the public's understanding of current policy dilemmas. CSRs are written by individual authors—who may be Council Fellows or acknowledged experts from outside the institution—in consultation with an advisory committee, and are intended to take sixty days from inception to publication. The committee serves as a sounding board and provides feedback on a draft report. It usually meets twice— once before a draft is written and once again when there is a draft for review; however, advisory committee members, unlike Task Force members, are not asked to sign off on the report or to otherwise endorse it. Once published, CSRs are posted on the Council's website, CFR.org.

For further information about the Council or this Special Report, please write to the Council on Foreign Relations, 58 East 68th Street, New York, NY 10021, or call the Communications office at 212-434-9888. Visit our website, CFR.org.

To submit a letter in response to a Council Special Report for publication on our website, CFR.org, you may send an email to CSReditor@cfr.org. Alternatively, letters may be mailed to us at: Publications Department, Council on Foreign Relations, 58 East 68th Street, New York, NY 10021. Letters should include the writer's name, postal address, and daytime phone number. Letters may be edited for length and clarity, and may be published online. Please do not send attachments. All letters become the property of the Council on Foreign Relations and will not be returned. We regret that, owing to the volume of correspondence, we cannot respond to every letter.

CONTENTS

FOREWORD

The International Monetary Fund's purpose and scope of work have changed dramatically since its founding after World War II. Whereas at first the Fund aimed to maintain monetary and exchange-rate stability among a mostly industrialized membership, today most members are developing countries, ranging from large, emerging markets to small, impoverished states. The Fund's surveillance of macroeconomic issues has expanded to cover topics with little direct relevance to its mandate. Moreover, though no industrialized country has drawn on the Fund for more than twenty years, such countries still dominate the Fund's decision-making.

These developments have sparked calls for reform. Proposals to modify the Fund's activities, lending facilities, and governance have come from many experts, including the Fund's managing director. Others, who find the Fund illegitimate or obsolete, have called for its abolition. This Council Special Report, written by Peter B. Kenen under the auspices of the Council's Maurice R. Greenberg Center for Geoeconomic Studies, rejects the urgings of the abolitionists and goes on to contend that efforts to reform the Fund deserve U.S. support. Many countries remain at risk for financial crises, and a strong Fund that can take the lead in responding is in the U.S. interest. With well-managed reform, the Fund could also play a useful role in resolving global economic imbalances. Overall, the report argues, the United States should not try to achieve unilaterally what the Fund can and should achieve multilaterally.

In making this case, Dr. Kenen offers a balanced assessment of the managing director's reform proposals in both the Fund's substantive areas of work and its governance—endorsing some, criticizing others, and urging a more aggressive role in confronting global imbalances. *Reform of the International Monetary Fund* demonstrates that with reasonable reform of its activities and structures, the Fund can remain relevant to the pressing global economic challenges we face.

Richard N. Haass
President
Council on Foreign Relations
May 2007

ACKNOWLEDGMENTS

I am grateful to Douglas Holtz-Eakin, the previous director of the Maurice R. Greenberg Center for Geoeconomic Studies, and to his successor, Sebastian Mallaby, for giving me the opportunity to write this Council Special Report. I am likewise grateful to the members of the Council on Foreign Relations advisory committee for their careful reading of the outline and first draft of the manuscript and their constructive comments: Caroline Atkinson, Nancy Birdsall, James Boughton, Elaine Buckberg, Andrew Crockett, Kristin J. Forbes, David D. Hale, Douglas Holtz-Eakin, Yves-Andre Istel, Brad W. Setser, Amity R. Shlaes, Kathleen Stephansen, Daniel K. Tarullo, Edwin M. Truman, and Christine I. Wallich. Jeffrey R. Shafer chaired the committee firmly but graciously, and I am deeply indebted to him. Special thanks go to those committee members who gave me written comments on the manuscript, improving it in many ways and sparing me some outright errors. The same special thanks go to Stanley Fischer and Sebastian Mallaby for reading the manuscript and giving me thoughtful written comments. None of them, however, bears responsibility for the views expressed in this report.

I also thank Richard N. Haass, president of the Council on Foreign Relations, James M. Lindsay, the director of Studies when this project got under way, and Gary Samore, his successor, for their guidance and encouragement. The timely appearance of this report also owes much to Patricia Dorff and Lia Norton in the Council's Publications department, Anya Schememann and her team in Communications, and Jessica Legnos, program coordinator in the Council's Studies department. Finally, I am grateful to Laura Little, the research associate on this project, for tracking down documents and data and for putting the manuscript in final form.

Peter B. Kenen

ACRONYMS

ED	Executive Directors
EFF	Extended Fund Facility
EU	European Union
GDP	gross domestic product
G7	Group of Seven
HIPC	Heavily Indebted Poor Countries
IMF	International Monetary Fund, the Fund
IMFC	International Monetary and Financial Committee
PPP	purchasing power parity
PRGF	Poverty Reduction and Growth Facility
SBA	standby arrangements
SRF	Supplemental Reserve Facility

COUNCIL SPECIAL REPORT

INTRODUCTION

The International Monetary Fund (IMF) is undertaking a wide-ranging reform of its governance and operations within a framework proposed by Rodrigo de Rato, its managing director. The proposed reform is inspired in large part by the emergence of large middle-income developing countries such as China and India, which now play a major role in the world economy but are underrepresented in the Fund as the low-income developing countries. The proposed reform is also inspired by the need to simplify the Fund's internal practices and focus more intensively on its basic mandate: to "oversee the development of the international monetary system in order to ensure its effective operation."[1]

This effort is overdue. The policies and practices of the Fund have evolved substantially in recent years, but too much of that evolution has involved the addition of new tasks that have burdened the Fund's executive board, its principal decision-making body, as well as the Fund's management and staff.

One may have reservations about some of the managing director's proposals and contemplate other ways of achieving his main objectives, and this Special Report will do that. It will, in fact, propose modifications in one of the innovations proposed by the managing director—the introduction of "multilateral surveillance" aimed at reducing the huge imbalances among the major countries—and will question the way that the Fund would determine countries' eligibility for access to a new "precautionary facility" to provide quasi-automatic financing to countries with sound policies.

Nevertheless, this Special Report will argue that the reform effort requires and deserves the support of the United States, including the U.S. Congress when it is asked to adopt the legislation required to implement some of the key measures. Without the support of the United States, no reform effort can possibly succeed. Without reform, moreover, the Fund may be ill-equipped to deal with financial crises of the sort that are virtually certain to occur in the future.

---

[1] International Monetary Fund, *Articles of Agreement*, Article IV(3a).

THE CASE FOR IMF REFORM

Has the IMF outlived its usefulness? Has it done more harm than good, as some of its critics claim?

Those who take the first view note that many middle-income developing countries have ample access to global financial markets and have accumulated large reserves that allow them to self-insure against any cessation or outright reversal of capital inflows. They also note that there have been no major crises for several years and that large numbers of emerging-market countries have built up large reserves with which they can deal with future crises. One has only to remember, however, how quickly and unexpectedly crises have developed in the past and how they have spread from one country to another. It would thus be imprudent to assume that there will be no crises in the future. On this view, of course, the case for speedy reform of the Fund takes on more strength, not less. It would be far harder to reform the Fund in the midst of a new crisis than to do so now. It is easier to modernize a fire brigade when there are few fires than in the midst of a major conflagration.

Those who take the second view charge that the Fund creates moral hazard: It encourages borrowing countries to take on excessive debt, knowing that the Fund will come to their rescue, and it also encourages foreign investors to lend too freely to developing countries, believing that that they will be bailed out in the event of a crisis. They also claim that Fund lending is heavily subsidized by the taxpayers of the developed countries, because interest rates on IMF lending are much lower than the market interest rates at which developing countries can borrow.[2] Some of these critics also believe that the Fund's advice has been seriously flawed.[3]

---

[2] Adam Lerrick, "Funding the IMF: How Much Does It Really Cost?" *Quarterly International Economics Report,* November 2003, and the more eclectic treatment of the subject by Desmond Lachman, in Edwin M. Truman, ed., *Reforming the IMF for the 21st Century* (Washington, DC: Institute for International Economics, 2006), Ch. 23.

[3] Allan H. Meltzer, "New Mandates for the IMF and World Bank," *Cato Journal,* Winter 2005, pp.13–16.

There is some truth to the moral-hazard argument; any form of insurance, including the expectation of financing from the IMF, may raise the risk of imprudent behavior by those having it. This was surely true in Russia in the lead-up to its default in 1998.[4] But the domestic political cost of having to ask the Fund for help surely reduces the risk of imprudent behavior. On the lenders' side, moreover, the losses incurred by holders of Russian and Argentine debt have reduced the risk of imprudent behavior by foreign lenders.

There is likewise some truth to the claim that Fund lending is subsidized by the taxpayers of the industrial countries. The interest rate paid by the Fund on its use of its members' contributions is lower than the long-term interest rates that the industrial countries pay on their own national debts. But the more extravagant version of the argument is blatantly wrong. It compares the interest rate that countries must pay on their drawing from the Fund with the interest rate they would have to pay to private lenders. The latter, of course, is much higher, especially at times of crisis—which is when countries go to the Fund. But this difference in borrowing costs does not constitute quite the subsidy that critics claim, because the Fund is a preferred creditor. The Fund must be repaid before private creditors, and can safely charge a lower interest rate than private creditors, which run a greater risk of default and thus seek larger compensation for that greater risk. Moreover, the difference between the rate charged by private lenders and by the IMF does not constitute a burden on the taxpayers of the developed countries.

Although IMF bailouts involve modest costs to taxpayers, and although their availability creates some moral hazard, the importance of the IMF to the interests of the United States can be gauged by imagining a world without the Fund. What could the United States do on its own if a country of particular importance, such as Pakistan or South Africa, ran into serious trouble—a sudden cessation of capital inflows, a sharp depreciation of its home currency, and risk of default on its external debt? Any disruption of international financial markets, regardless of its cause or origin, could have serious adverse effects on the originating, emerging-market country as well as other countries,

---

[4] Michael D. Bordo and Harold James, "The International Monetary Fund: Its Present Role in Historical Perspective," National Bureau of Economic Research Working Paper No. 7724, June 2004, especially pp. 39–40.

despite the steps such countries have taken to strengthen their financial systems and the very large foreign-exchange reserves that many of them now hold.

Could the United States, acting unilaterally, provide such countries with the funding they would need to ride out a crisis? Could it impose unilaterally the sorts of policy conditions that the IMF imposes when a country seeks its help? It would not be impossible, but it would be costly. It would assuredly foment the wrath of the public in the afflicted country—the same sort of anger often aimed at the IMF when it requires changes in a country's policies that are painful economically and politically.

Although the legitimacy of the IMF has been impaired by the inadequate representation of the developing countries, and the Fund has made some serious mistakes, it is nevertheless obliged to require its members to undertake unpopular reforms when they seek its help. The United States would pay a high political price if it took on that role, even if it limited its intervention to a handful of key countries. Much of the world is angry with the United States. It would be imprudent for it to foster more hostility by acting unilaterally to rescue crisis countries. The Fund can more readily afford to insist on unpopular policy changes to the extent that its dealings with its members cover a limited range of issues. The United States cannot intervene and insist so easily because of its manifold interests in so many countries, including importantly strategic interests, as well as wide-ranging economic interests.

There are, in addition, two practical problems:

First, would the U.S. Congress be willing and able to act promptly if asked to appropriate the large amount of money required to combat a financial crisis, even in a country of obvious importance to the United States? Recall what happened after the Mexican crisis of 1994. When Congress declined to approve a loan guarantee to Mexico, the U.S. Treasury used the Exchange Stabilization Fund—the Treasury's principal vehicle for providing bilateral aid to troubled countries—in order to make a large loan to Mexico jointly with the IMF. In August 1995, however, Congress adopted legislation, the so-called D'Amato amendment, which restricted the Treasury's future use of the Exchange Stabilization Fund without congressional approval. Although that legislation lapsed two years later, it inhibited the United States from helping Thailand in 1997 and allowed Japan to take the lead in providing bilateral aid to Thailand, thereby leaving a residue of resentment against the United States. But even if Congress were willing to act, could it act promptly enough to contain a crisis in a major foreign country? And might not it be tempted to attach extraneous conditions to such aid, including demands for improved labor standards or trade-policy changes?

Second, the Fund's staff is far smaller than that of the World Bank; it has fewer than three thousand employees, compared with some ten thousand at the World Bank. Yet, the Fund's staff is far larger than the international staff of the U.S. Treasury. The Fund can thus monitor developments in its member countries in a manner that would be far more difficult for the U.S. Treasury to accomplish, even with the aid of other U.S. government agencies. Crises develop quickly, sometimes without warning, and the Fund knows a lot more about its member countries than the United States, thanks partly to its regular surveillance of those countries. The Fund is therefore far better placed than the U.S. Treasury to design a package of policy reforms when a country seeks its help.

The Fund is often portrayed as an instrument of U.S. policy because the United States is by far its most influential member. Far better, however, to be accused of using the Fund to achieve the objectives of U.S. policy than having to act unilaterally to combat international financial crises.[5]

The premise of this report is therefore that the United States has an interest in a healthy IMF that can take the lead in managing financial crises. Even though there have been no such crises since the default of Argentina in 2001, history teaches us that there will be more in the future. But in addition to crisis lending, the IMF may also play a role in managing other strains in the international system.

Most developing countries are not yet fully integrated into the global economy, but some are being drawn into it far faster than we would have forecast a few years ago. We are thus close to having a single world market for goods, services, and capital, and, as its monetary counterpart, a single world market for national currencies. What happens in the monetary market, moreover, is increasingly influenced by the national policies of many countries, not just the major developed countries. China's economic policies affect

---

[5] The same point is made by Henning, who nonetheless observes that the United States may need to use the Exchange Stabilization Fund in tandem with the IMF, as it did in the Mexican case. He argues, however, that the Fund should set the policy conditions; see C. Randall Henning, *The Exchange Stabilization Fund: Slush Money or War Chest* (Washington, DC: Institute for International Economics, 1999).

the value of the dollar, not just vis-à-vis the renminbi, but likewise vis-à-vis the euro, yen, and other major currencies. Yet, global integration does not automatically lead to global cooperation. Global cooperation is threatened by the growth of regional arrangements, especially in trade, but likewise in monetary and financial matters. Cooperation is also threatened by a common tendency to insist that the task of rectifying international imbalances resides with other governments, not with all of them together.

It is, therefore, essential that there be a worldwide acceptance of certain basic principles. It must be recognized, for example, that no country's exchange rate is the exclusive property of that single country. The dollar-yen exchange rate is likewise the yen-dollar rate, and it must also be recognized that one country's policies, including its fiscal and monetary policies, constrain the policy choices of others. In the words of the Fund's Articles of Agreement, there is a manifest need "to promote international monetary cooperation through a permanent institution which provides the machinery for consultation and collaboration on international monetary problems."[6]

No such institution, however, can do its job unless the vast majority of its members believe their concerns are given respectful attention. Absent that conviction, the institution will lack the legitimacy required to influence its members' behavior in ways that promote general, global welfare. Likewise, an institution will lack legitimacy if its members believe that it is dominated by a handful of large countries mindful of only their own immediate interests—and that is the principal risk facing the Fund.

There is a twofold case for reforms to strengthen the governance and legitimacy of the Fund: to ready it for future emerging-market crises and to increase the chances that it can contribute to the orderly resolution of global imbalances.

---

[6] International Monetary Fund. *Articles of Agreement*, Article I(i).

THE EVOLUTION AND STRUCTURE OF THE FUND

To understand and evaluate the reforms proposed by the managing director, it is worth reviewing briefly the evolution and present structure of the Fund.

Created in 1944, the International Monetary Fund was meant to govern and support the international monetary system in the postwar world. It was designed to prevent a repetition of the disorderly exchange-rate changes of the 1930s and provide its members with temporary financing when they encountered balance-of-payments problems. It also committed its members to move as rapidly as possible to current-account convertibility—the elimination of restrictions on external payments arising from trade in goods and services—although it allowed them to retain restrictions on international capital flows.

Under the Fund's Articles of Agreement, its constitution, each member of the Fund was obliged to maintain a fixed exchange rate defined in terms of gold or the U.S. dollar unless it faced a "fundamental disequilibrium" in its balance of payments, in which case it could alter its exchange rate. The Fund, in turn, would provide temporary financing to a member facing severe difficulty defending its exchange rate. The Fund is not a bank; it cannot create money. It is sometimes described as being analogous to a credit union.[7] Each member government makes financial resources available to the IMF, largely in its own national currency, and receives in return the right to receive financial assistance from the Fund as well as the right to vote in its decision-making bodies.[8]

To this end, each member is assigned a quota based on a formula aimed to reflect its ability to provide financial resources to the Fund and its potential vulnerability to balance-of-payments problems. Its quota plays a triple role: It sets the size of each member's contribution to the Fund's financial resources, governs the amount that a member can draw on those resources, and determines the member's voting power in the

---

[7] Peter B. Kenen, *Financing, Adjustment, and the International Monetary Fund* (Washington, DC: The Brookings Institution, 1986).
[8] Each country was given an equal number of so-called basic votes (the number of which has not changed since the IMF was founded). It was also given additional votes geared to the size of its quota, discussed next in the text. Quotas must be reviewed every five years and have been increased several times. For the most part, however, the increases in quotas have been proportional to the countries' existing quotas.

9

Fund's two governing bodies, its board of governors and its executive board. A third body, the International Monetary and Financial Committee (IMFC), was established much later to oversee the work of the Fund and make recommendations to the board of governors, the executive board, and the Fund's management. The managing director of the Fund chairs the executive board and directs the work of the Fund's staff.

Under the Fund's Articles of Agreement, the executive board is supposed to have twenty members, but that number can be raised or lowered if members casting at least 85 percent of the total voting power vote to do that, and there are now twenty-four executive directors. Some executive directors represent individual countries, including the United States, which, by itself, has nearly 17 percent of the total voting power—enough to block a decision to change the size of the board and also to block a number of other important decisions, including decisions to change total quotas and to amend the Articles of Agreement. (The other individual countries with seats on the board are Japan, Germany, France, the United Kingdom, Saudi Arabia, China, and Russia.) The rest of the 177 member countries are grouped into sixteen multicountry constituencies, each of which has an executive director who casts the votes of all the countries in his or her constituency (see Table 1).

It is fairly safe to say that the U.S. voting share will never fall below 15 percent of the total voting power in the IMF without the consent of the United States. Such a change would deprive the United States of its ability to block decisions requiring an 85 percent majority, including decisions to change Fund quotas and to amend the Fund's Articles of Agreement. It is, in fact, nearly impossible to strip the United States of that blocking power, because the same 85 percent majority is needed to approve an increase or redistribution of IMF quotas.

It should also be noted that U.S. participation in the Fund is governed by the Bretton Woods Agreement Act, not by a treaty, and that U.S. quota increases are treated as appropriations, although they are not treated as budgetary outlays because they represent an exchange of assets between the United States and the Fund. Therefore, both the Senate and the House of Representatives must approve all decisions involving increased U.S. participation in the Fund, and they would be sure to reject any change in the distribution of IMF quotas that deprived the United States of its ability to block those

Table 1: Executive Directors (EDs) and Voting Shares			
Nationality of ED	**Countries in Constituency**	**Percentages of Total Votes**	**Four Countries with Largest Number of Votes**
Appointed:			
United States	1	16.83	X
Japan	1	6.04	X
Germany	1	5.90	X
France	1	4.87	X
United Kingdom	1	4.87	X
Other Single-Country Constituencies:			
China	1	3.67	X
Saudi Arabia	1	3.17	X
Russia	1	2.70	X
Elected (Multicountry) Constituencies:			
Belgium	10	5.16	Belgium, Austria, Turkey, Hungary
Netherlands	12	4.77	Netherlands, Ukraine, Romania, Israel
Venezuela	8	4.21	Spain, Mexico, Venezuela, Guatemala
Italy	7	4.12	Italy, Portugal, Greece, Malta
Australia	14	3.87	Australia, Korea, New Zealand, Philippines
Canada	12	3.65	Canada, Ireland, Jamaica, Bahamas
Finland	8	3.45	Sweden, Denmark, Norway, Finland
Egypt	13	3.21	Kuwait, Iraq, Libya, Egypt
Indonesia	12	3.13	Indonesia, Malaysia, Thailand, Singapore
Kenya	19	2.95	South Africa, Nigeria, Zambia, Angola
Switzerland	8	2.80	Switzerland, Poland, Serbia, Uzbekistan
Iran	7	2.43	Iran, Algeria, Pakistan, Morocco
Brazil	9	2.43	Brazil, Colombia, Trinidad & Tobago, Ecuador
India	4	2.36	India, Bangladesh, Sri Lanka, Bhutan
Peru	6	1.96	Argentina, Chile, Peru, Uruguay
Rwanda	24	1.39	Dem. Rep. of Congo, Cote d'Ivore, Cameroon, Senegal
Total	181*	99.97**	

*Total does not include votes of Somalia, which did not participate in the 2006 election of executive directors, nor Liberia and Zimbabwe, whose votes have been suspended. Montenegro is also omitted, having been admitted to the Fund too late to be included in this data set.

**Detail may not add to total because of rounding.

critical decisions.[9] It should also be noted, however, that the United States is not overrepresented in the Fund. By almost any measure one might use, including gross domestic product (GDP), as well as the formulas actually used to compute so-called calculated quotas, the United States is underrepresented.

The European Union (EU), by contrast, is overrepresented. In addition to the three chairs held by executive directors appointed by individual EU countries, four of the multicountry constituencies in the executive board are led by representatives of EU countries, and other EU countries, such as Spain, are influential members of additional constituencies. Furthermore, every managing director of the Fund has been European and every president of the World Bank has been American.

The Fund's membership was quite small initially, but it increased hugely in the 1960s and 1970s due to decolonization and again in the 1990s due to the disintegration of the Soviet empire. There are 185 members today. Moreover, in the early years, some major industrial countries drew on the financial resources of the Fund, but none has done so for decades. The result has been a de facto division of the Fund into two groups: the industrial countries, which dominate decision-making, and the developing countries, many of which are the clients of the Fund. That has tended to undermine the analogy with a credit union.

The system of fixed exchange rates that was central to the functioning of the Fund collapsed at the start of the 1970s, with the move to floating exchange rates by the major industrial countries, and the Articles of Agreement were amended accordingly. Article IV of the amended Articles permitted each member to adopt the exchange-rate regime it preferred but conferred upon the Fund itself the task of overseeing the international monetary system. It instructed the Fund to exercise "firm surveillance over the exchange rate policies of members" and to "adopt specific principles for the guidance of all members with respect to those policies."[10]

---

[9] On the congressional politics of IMF-related legislation, see J. Lawrence Broz, "Changing IMF Quotas: The Role of the United States Congress," in Ariel Buira, ed., *Reforming the Governance of the IMF and the World Bank* (London: Anthem Press, 2005), Ch. 12.
[10] International Monetary Fund. *Articles of Agreement,* Article IV(3b).

In practice, Fund surveillance has been concerned with a wide range of national policies, and the same tendency has been manifest in IMF conditionality—the policy changes that the Fund requires of countries that seek to borrow from it.

There is no explicit basis for conditionality in the Articles of Agreement, but the managing director is required to assure the executive board that a country borrowing from the Fund will be able to repay the debt and will thus adopt the policies necessary for that purpose. Over the years, however, conditionality was gradually extended to include large numbers of national policies having little or no bearing on a country's ability to repay the Fund. This tendency was illustrated vividly by the very long lists of conditions included in IMF programs during the Asian crisis of the late 1990s, which were deeply resented in Asia.

The Fund has since decided, however, that "structural" conditions should not be included in IMF programs unless they are essential for achieving the programs' main macroeconomic objectives. The Asian episode, however, has had long-lasting effects. It catalyzed the efforts of Asian countries to build up their reserves and undertake regional cooperation in monetary matters, and it was likewise a stimulus to calls for IMF reform aimed at giving developing countries a bigger role in IMF decision-making, including especially the larger emerging-market countries.

THE FACILITIES OF THE FUND

Today there are four main ways in which a member country can draw on the Fund. The first three involve drawing on the quota-based resources of the institution. The first and most common is the standby arrangement (SBA); the second is the Extended Fund Facility (EFF), which provides longer-term financing to countries that face the need to undertake major reforms before they will be ready to repay the Fund; the third is the Supplemental Reserve Facility (SRF), which provides much larger amounts of short-term financing to countries that face a sudden and large reversal of foreign capital inflows. The fourth is the Poverty Reduction and Growth Facility (PRGF), which makes longer-term, low-interest loans to low-income developing countries, using money lent to the IMF by other member countries. These loans yield no net income to the Fund itself.

Some countries, however, have had difficulty repaying the PRGF, and some have used new PRGF loans to repay old ones. Furthermore, many of the existing loans have been or will be forgiven pursuant to the debt-relief initiative adopted by the Cologne Group of Seven (G7) Summit in 1999 and the Gleneagles G7 Summit in 2006. This decision has raised two questions: One, should low-income countries be allowed to build up new debts to the Fund? And two, is the Fund properly staffed to engage in lending aimed at promoting economic development and poverty reduction? Some have suggested that the PRGF and the processes associated with it should be transferred to the World Bank, which has the financial and human resources to focus on these countries' deep-seated problems.[11]

That is unlikely to happen, however, if only because one main aim of IMF reform is to give developing countries, including the low-income countries, more influence and ownership of the IMF, and they will continue to insist that the Fund play a role in combating poverty. It is clear, moreover, that low-income countries will continue to need balance-of payments financing from the international community, whether it comes from the Fund or the Bank, but that would not be precluded by transferring the PRGF to the Bank. The low-income countries could still draw on the ordinary facilities of the Fund, although the interest payments on those drawings might have to be subsidized by the developed countries.[12]

---

[11] Michael Mussa and Tommaso Padoa-Schioppa take the same view in Edwin M. Truman, ed., *Reforming the IMF for the 21st Century* (Washington, DC: Institute for International Economics, 2006), Chs. 21 and 27. See also Timothy Lane, "Tension in the Role of the IMF and Directions for Reform," *World Economics* 6, April–June 2005, pp. 56–59; he would confine the Fund to an advisory role but does not explicitly propose that all concessional financing be provided by the World Bank.

[12] In a comprehensive report on collaboration between the IMF and World Bank, a group of experts chaired by Pedro Malan has made a similar suggestion. The Fund, it says, should gradually withdraw completely from long-term lending to the low-income countries. But the PRGF should remain in being so that the Fund can provide subsidized short-term balance-of-payments financing to those countries. The report makes many other recommendations designed to delineate more clearly the responsibilities of the Fund and Bank and improve coordination between them. See *Report of the External Review Committee on Bank—Fund Collaboration* (Washington, DC: International Monetary Fund and World Bank, 2007).

REFORMING THE FUND

It would be utterly imprudent to shut down the IMF. It would be equally imprudent, however, to deny the need for reforming the Fund. The Fund must be empowered to deal more effectively with the functioning of the whole monetary system in a manner consonant with its stated purpose—promoting international monetary cooperation and providing a venue for consultation and cooperation among its major members. That process has now begun, although the outcome is uncertain.

In September 2005, the managing director of the Fund, Rodrigo de Rato, issued a paper on what he described as the Fund's medium-term strategy. In April 2006, he issued a longer paper, "Implementing the Fund's Medium-Term Strategy,"[13] in which he proposed substantial changes in the governance and activities of the IMF. Here is a partial list of the changes he proposed:

- Reforming IMF surveillance of its member countries;
- Undertaking a new form of multilateral surveillance to assist in resolving systemic threats to the stability of the monetary system, including large global imbalances and currency misalignments;
- Reforming the distribution of IMF quotas and, therefore, voting power, to recognize the increased economic importance of emerging-market countries;
- Establishing a new Fund facility to provide precautionary financing for countries that have prudent policies but may nonetheless experience difficulties because of balance-sheet weaknesses and vulnerabilities;
- Reviewing the Fund's policies on "lending into arrears" when a country fails to service fully its debts to foreign creditors;
- Adopting a new way to choose the Fund's managing director.

---

[13] International Monetary Fund. *The Managing Director's Report on Implementing the Fund's Medium-Term Strategy* (Washington, DC, April 3, 2006), cited hereafter as *Managing Director's Report*. This essay focuses on the managing director's own proposals. For a superb, wide-ranging treatment of IMF reform, see Edwin M. Truman's chapters in Truman, ed., *Reforming the IMF,* Chs. 2, 9, and 29.

The managing director also promised the appointment of an external committee to find ways of increasing the Fund's own income, as the recent falloff of IMF lending has reduced its interest income, posing a serious budgetary problem that could force the Fund to curtail its activities absent a new and stable source of income. That committee, chaired by Andrew Crockett, published its report in January 2007 and made several recommendations, including one that will be controversial and may require the approval of the U.S. Congress—the sale of some of the Fund's gold holdings to create an income-producing endowment fund.[14]

REFORMING IMF SURVEILLANCE

The rationale for IMF surveillance resides in a passage quoted above, concerning Fund surveillance of its members' exchange-rate policies. Over the years, however, the scope of surveillance has been broadened. The annual reports prepared by staff missions now cover a host of issues, many of them having little direct relevance to the main mandate of the Fund. In the words of the managing director's report,

> surveillance has become procedural and diffuse, adapting over the years to new challenges by expanding its coverage from the original emphasis on exchange rates and macroeconomic policies to structural reforms, standards and codes, banking stability, social issues, and anti-money laundering. However, the complexity of globalization cannot be answered by ever longer and more complicated analysis. Rather, what is needed is focus on the essential, the framing of issues in a global context, and better use of the Fund's comparative advantage—its universal reach and macroeconomic expertise—to achieve progress on key issues.[15]

The reading and discussion of these voluminous reports puts an enormous burden on the executive board, which is swamped each year by some eighty-two thousand pages of

---

[14] International Monetary Fund, *Final Report of the Committee to Study Sustainable Financing of the IMF* (Washington, DC: International Monetary Fund, January 31, 2007).
[15] *Managing Director's Report*, pp. 2–3.

paper.[16] The managing director therefore proposed a streamlined approach to country surveillance, and this proposal has been adopted by the executive board. The Fund is no longer undertaking annual surveillance of many member countries, especially small, stable countries; it is moving instead to biennial surveillance of them. It is also reducing the coverage of surveillance to focus on subjects of central concern to the Fund. There is little point in producing voluminous annual reports on countries where conditions have not changed substantially and do not pose a threat to the country's own stability or that of any other country. The managing director also proposed that surveillance play closer attention to financial and balance-sheet vulnerabilities, as they have played a major role in most emerging-market crises. Most importantly, he proposed that more emphasis be given to the original aim of surveillance—assessing the consistency of exchange-rate and macroeconomic policies with national and international stability.[17]

---

[16] The number of pages of paper, moreover, tells only part of the story. Consider this list of tasks imposed on the executive director who represents the twenty-four-country African constituency:

> [I]n the 24-country African constituency within the IMF, some 21 countries are IDA eligible (very low income). If we assume that all are within PRGF supported programs, the Executive Director's office should be involved in some 42 on-site missions which present PRGF semi-annual reviews to the Executive Board. On top of this, there is the work required to prepare 24 countries' Article IV consultations (typically on an annual basis) ... Further to this work, since most countries (21 out of 24) are eligible for debt relief under the HIPC Initiative, the Executive Director and other officials will also have to prepare for considerations by the Board ... documents of the respective countries as they progress under the initiative. On top of all this, there are field missions for those members undertaking a voluntary assessment of international standards, other missions relating to Financial Sector Assessment Programs, as well as possible technical assistance missions. Importantly, this exercise only takes into account duties related to the Executive Director holding the chair of the constituency that elected them *and does not consider the heavier workload resulting from their being members* of the Executive Board which is '... responsible for conducting the business of the Fund...' (Woods, Ngaire, in Ariel Buira, ed., *Reforming the Governance of the IMF*, p. 154).

[17] To this end, the managing director has also suggested that the Consultative Group on Exchange Rates expand its remit to cover not only industrial countries but also twenty emerging-market countries, and this suggestion has already been adopted. The executive board is also reexamining the 1977 principles governing exchange-rate surveillance.

While country-by-country surveillance reports, appropriately limited in frequency and scope, are very useful, they cannot readily grapple with global imbalances involving the world's largest countries. Addressing this problem, the managing director has proposed a new form of surveillance—a process of multilateral surveillance aimed at achieving the mutual adjustment of those countries' policies.

There has been much discussion of the need for this sort of adjustment, including bilateral consultations between U.S. and Chinese officials. But existing multilateral forums are not well structured for this purpose. The G7, comprising the main industrial countries (Canada, France, Germany, Italy, Japan, the United Kingdom, and the United States), does not include any of the large emerging-market countries, although the leaders of those countries have sometimes been invited to meet informally with the heads of government of the G7 countries at the annual G7 Summit. But the Fund has played no major role in these consultations, nor can it require policy changes by the countries jointly responsible for the huge global imbalances that threaten the stability of the world economy. It cannot compel China to revalue its currency nor insist that the United States reduce its budget deficit.

The managing director has therefore proposed a new multilateral consultation process. It would begin—it has indeed begun—with bilateral consultations between the staff of the Fund and each of the principal countries involved, followed by multilateral meetings with those same countries. The staff of the Fund will then draft a report to be discussed by the executive board of the Fund and, ultimately, the IMFC.

The managing director has not proposed that the staff make specific country-by-country recommendations to the executive board and IMFC. At some point in the future, however, the staff of the Fund should publish its findings and policy recommendations, even without the endorsement of the executive board or IMFC—a strategy more radical than the one proposed by the managing director. To cut the process short without the publication of the staff's findings and recommendations would gravely reduce the effectiveness of the whole process. It is unrealistic to expect that the executive board and IMFC will agree on the steps that should be taken by the key countries involved. Those bodies are too likely to issue anodyne declarations devoid of incisive policy recommendations, because operational recommendations are bound to provoke dissent by one or more of the countries involved in the multilateral consultations.[18]

Although the Fund cannot compel acceptance of the staff's findings and recommendations, the process could still be productive if it could help stimulate domestic debate within the countries involved where there are, even now, divergent views about the appropriate policy changes. The success of the process, however, will surely depend on the staff's ability to make its own recommendations rather than listen to national governments say what they have said before and then merely summarize that. It will also depend on the countries' respect for the independence of the staff and on the staff's ability to display an understanding of the problems and constraints that face the countries involved.

Multilateral surveillance is no panacea but holds out hope of progress, not only in framing the key issues and getting the adjustment process going but in managing the process once it is under way and avoiding an abrupt, disruptive correction of the huge imbalances among the major countries, which could gravely impair the role of the dollar as the world's preeminent currency. It may indeed be the only coherent strategy for achieving an orderly reduction in those imbalances. Its success, however, will depend importantly on the willingness of each government involved to say what it would be willing to do if the other participants did likewise. Too much of the debate about global imbalances has been marred by the tendency of each government to tell the other

---

[18] The IMFC may find it hard to reach agreement on recommendations more specific than those in the communiqué it issued at the Singapore meeting on September 17, 2006:

> The Committee calls for sustained action to implement the agreed policy strategy to underpin an orderly unwinding of global imbalances. The strategy involves: steps to boost national saving in the United States, including fiscal consolidation; further progress on growth-enhancing reforms in Europe; further structural reforms, including fiscal consolidation in Japan; reforms to boost domestic demand in emerging Asia, together with greater exchange rate flexibility in a number of surplus countries; and increased spending consistent with absorptive capacity and macroeconomic stability in oil producing countries.

governments what *they* should do, rather than indicate what it would contribute to a package of policy changes.

During the first round of multilateral consultations, each participating country listed the policy changes it was prepared to make. Yet most of the cited policy changes appeared to reflect decisions the countries had already unilaterally made rather than new commitments produced during the consultations themselves. China, for example, promised to "improve the exchange rate formation mechanism in a gradual and controllable manner" with the aim of achieving a gradual increase in exchange-rate flexibility relative to a basket of currencies, but China said nothing about the time it would take to achieve this objective. Similarly, the fiscal commitments offered by the United States were those already contained in the president's budget proposal for fiscal 2008.[19]

It is perhaps too early to conclude that multilateral surveillance in its present form can make only a marginal contribution to the rectification of global imbalances. The approach seemingly favored by the U.S. Treasury—an ongoing bilateral dialogue between Beijing and Washington covering all of the issues outstanding between them—may be more effective in the present case. Yet having the IMF staff make its own policy recommendations to the governments involved, as proposed above, might make it somewhat harder for those governments to claim that their existing or planned policies constitute substantial contributions to the resolution of global imbalances.

REFORMING THE GOVERNANCE OF THE FUND

The formula used when the Fund was established, the so-called Bretton Woods formula, is still used in calculating the IMF quota shares of individual countries, but four other formulas are used as well. A country's calculated quota share is then set at the larger of two numbers: the current value given by the original Bretton Woods formula and the average of the values of two more—the two of the four other formulas that yield the

---

[19] See International Monetary Fund, *International Monetary and Financial Committee Reviews Multilateral Consultation,* IMF Press Release 07/72, Washington, DC, April 14, 2007.

lowest values.[20] Actual quota shares, however, differ substantially from calculated shares. When total quotas have been increased, most of the increase has been used to provide an equi-proportional increase in each country's quota, rather than one based on the current value of its calculated quota. Furthermore, no attempt has been made to increase the number of so-called basic votes, which remain at the level (250 per member) that they were when the Fund was established, and they have thus shrunk rather sharply relative to quota-based votes, to the disadvantage of members with small quotas.

Therefore, the managing director has proposed and the governors have approved a two-stage process. In the first stage, four countries (China, Korea, Mexico, and Turkey) with actual quotas far smaller than their economic weight will receive immediate though small increases in their quotas. This change was agreed to at the Singapore meeting of the Fund in September 2006. In the second stage, which is supposed to take place in mid-2008, the Fund would adopt a new formula for calculating quotas and then enact another round of increases for countries that are still underrepresented relative to their newly calculated quotas. This process could lead to a substantial redistribution of voting power in the IMF, depending on the nature of the new formula and the rigor with which it is applied. (Under the Fund's Articles of Agreement, however, no country can be compelled to accept an absolute reduction in its quota without its consent; although a country's share in total quotas can, of course, be reduced if its quota is raised by less than that of other countries.)

The managing director has made no proposal of his own regarding reform of the quota formula, and it will not be easy to reach agreement on a new formula. The United States favors a formula that would give predominant weight to GDP, but many other countries favor one that would continue to give weight to other variables of the sort included in the existing formulas—those that reflect the openness of a member country and its vulnerability to external shocks.[21] The managing director did propose a substantial

---

[20] At each step in the process, however, the numbers produced by the formulas are adjusted to make sure that the sum of all countries' calculated quotas equals the desired level of total quotas. For details, see International Monetary Fund, *Quotas—Updated Calculations,* Washington, DC, 2004.

[21] Laura dos Reis, "Measuring Vulnerability: Capital Flows Volatility in the Quota Formula," in Ariel Buira, ed., *Reforming the Governance of the IMF and World Bank,* Ch. 8. There is, in addition, a debate between those who would measure GDP at current market exchange rates and those who would measure it at purchasing power parity (PPP). The latter would give more weight to developing countries, where the

increase of basic votes to strengthen the representation of the smallest countries, and the 2006 Singapore meeting of the governors endorsed that proposal.[22] It is important, however, that basic votes be raised whenever quotas are raised; otherwise, the voting power of the smallest countries will shrink as it has in the past.

A new way to calculate countries' quotas, especially one that gave predominant weight to GDP, would assuredly increase the quota shares of the United States and other large countries and thus raise their voting power. But the United States has already indicated that it will forgo any increase in its *share* of total votes. It will be content with an increase in its quota that would preserve its present share, which is, as we saw, sufficient for it to block any decision requiring an 85 percent majority—including a decision to amend the Fund's Articles of Agreement.

If, then, there is to be a relative redistribution of quotas and votes, which countries' shares must fall? The members of the European Union are the most obvious candidates, whether measured by the size of their quotas or the number of seats on the executive board held or dominated by EU countries.[23] There are two ways to achieve this result: (1) The EU countries could form a single multicountry constituency, with the representation of that constituency rotating among the EU countries, and (2) the EU or euro-zone countries could seek to be recognized as a single entity eligible for membership in the IMF and then accept a single EU seat on the executive board.[24]

---

market prices of many goods are lower than those in developed countries, and adjustment for these price differences would raise the measured GDP of those countries. On this issue, see Ariel Buira and John B. McLenaghan, in Ariel Buira, ed., *Reforming the Governance of the IMF and World Bank,* Chs. 2 and 7; also Vijay Kelkar, et al. in Ariel Buira, ed., Ch. 3, who make a more radical suggestion: Quota contributions should be based on GDP at PPP, access to financing should be based on need, and voting rights should be based on a weighted average of quota contributions and the Westphalian principle (i.e., one country, one vote). Others have also suggested a double voting system, under which decisions would be taken only if approved by the appropriate majority of quota-based votes and a simple majority of the Fund's membership. For a thoughtful critique of the underlying issues, based on John Rawls's theory of justice, see Abbas Mirakhor and Zaida Iqbal, "Rethinking the Governance of the International Monetary Fund," IMF Working Paper WP/06/273, December 2006.

[22] This decision, however, will require an amendment to the Articles of Agreement and thus the endorsement of the U.S. Congress.

[23] In 2006, EU countries held three single-country seats on the executive board, accounting for 15.64 percent of the total votes, and four EU countries (Belgium, the Netherlands, Italy, and Finland) represented multicountry constituencies with 17.50 percent of the total votes. In three more multicountry constituencies, moreover, EU countries were among the largest in terms of voting power. See Table 1.

[24] On the issues involved in EU representation, see Lorenzo Bini Smaghi, "IMF Governance and the Political Economy of a Consolidated European Seat," in Edwin M. Truman, ed., *Reforming the IMF for the*

Both of these solutions, however, would presumably require an amendment to the Articles of Agreement. Under the present Articles, five members of the executive board "shall be appointed by the five members having the largest quotas"[25] and three of those five are at present EU countries (France, Germany, and the United Kingdom). Hence, those countries could not now join a single EU constituency. Furthermore, the Fund's members are sovereign states, and the EU is not. To complicate matters, the EU countries, including those that lead multicountry constituencies, have more than 15 percent of the total votes on the executive board, and they would thus have the power to block any change in the distribution of quotas that was not to their liking.[26]

There is another intractable problem involving the EU countries. Several of those countries, most notably the smaller ones, oppose any change in the quota formula, let alone consolidation of the EU's quotas, and they may have enough votes to block any change in the quota formula. The ultimate success of quota reform may thus depend on the willingness and ability of the larger EU countries to quell that opposition.

The problem of EU representation intersects with another, not discussed in the managing director's report. It is the size of the executive board. The Fund's Articles of Agreement say that there should be twenty executive directors, but the board itself may decide by an 85 percent vote to raise or reduce the number, and there are currently twenty-four executive directors. A board with only twenty members may be too large for the efficient conduct of business, and one with twenty-four is surely too large. It would be difficult, however, to reduce the size of the board, even to return to twenty members, without unifying EU representation. Several multicountry constituencies are already quite

---

21ˢᵗ Century, Ch. 10 and Lorenzo Bini Smaghi, "A Single EU Seat in the IMF?" *Journal of Common Market Studies* 42, pp. 229–48, June 2004.; also Géraldine Mahieu, Dirk Ooms, and Stéphanie Rotter, "The Governance of the International Monetary Fund with a Single EU Chair," *Financial Stability Review of the National Bank of Belgium* (June 2003), pp. 173–88. Van Houtven argues, however, that mixed constituencies like those containing EU countries serve as a "bridge" between the industrial and developing countries; see Leo Van Houtven, *Governance of the IMF* (Washington, DC: International Monetary Fund Pamphlet Series No. 53, August 2002), p. 68.

[25] International Monetary Fund, *Articles of Agreement*, Article XII(b).

[26] Another solution to the problem of EU representation would be an amendment to the Articles of Agreement allowing the consolidated representation of the members of a monetary union. This would change the juridical nature of the Fund, but would make a great deal of economic sense, as the members of a monetary union have a single currency and thus a single exchange rate. It would create new problems, however, because monetary unions do not have common fiscal policies nor common regimes for prudential supervision of their financial systems.

large and could not be merged with others without hugely increasing the workload of their executive directors. It would be possible and sensible to collect the twenty-seven EU members into six constituencies (one each for Germany, France, and the United Kingdom and three multicountry constituencies for the other twenty-four). But the results of one such attempt, shown in the Appendix to this Special Report, were disappointing; it reduced by only one the total number of constituencies, from twenty-four to twenty-three.

Although the IMF governors agreed that work on a new quota formula should be completed no later than the spring of 2008, agreement may be hard to reach, and the implementation of that agreement, increasing selectively the quotas of countries with actual quotas significantly smaller than their newly calculated quotas, is likely to be controversial. Furthermore, the scope for relative redistribution will depend on the size of the overall increase in quotas, and many countries, including the EU countries, believe it should be small.

A start could be made, however, by adopting a new quota formula in 2008, the deadline set by the governors, and agreeing to a second round of ad hoc quota increases for countries with actual quotas smaller than those implied by their newly calculated quotas. Thereafter, total quotas could be increased gradually, with the bulk of each increase going to the underrepresented countries. But there must be a firm commitment to carry this process to its conclusion, not stop after a single round of ad hoc adjustments, even though it may take several years. There should also be a commitment to keep on raising the number of basic votes as total quotas rise.[27]

A NEW FUND FACILITY

Countries normally seek the Fund's help after they run into trouble, and then they have to negotiate the policy conditions that will be attached to their borrowing. The managing director has proposed the creation of a new "precautionary" Fund facility. It would be

---

[27] For an illustration of this two-step process, see Edwin M. Truman in Truman, ed., pp. 227–29. It should be noted that the Singapore meeting agreed on the need to keep raising the number of basic votes but did not adopt a formula for achieving it.

available to countries that have strong macroeconomic policies and sustainable debt burdens but are still vulnerable to crises because of their balance-sheet weaknesses and vulnerabilities. A country qualifying for access to the new facility would be able to make a very large drawing, up to 300 percent of its quota, which would be automatically available in a single up-front purchase and could be augmented thereafter upon subsequent review of the country's situation and its policy response to an emerging problem. Policy conditions might be attached to drawings on the new facility, but such conditions would target policies aimed at maintaining macroeconomic stability and reducing the country's vulnerabilities, rather than focusing in great detail on the country's immediate problem and the policies adopted to deal with it.

This is an attractive proposal, especially for emerging-market countries that fear contamination from a neighbor's problem or the effects of a tightening of international credit conditions. Nevertheless, it has one weakness, illustrated by an academic paper that worked with a simplified version of the plan.[28] Compiling debt data for thirty-four countries from 1991 through 2002, the authors found that the countries' ratios of debt to GDP and of budget deficits to GDP would have impaired the eligibility of eleven countries, temporarily or permanently, after they had qualified, and it would have precluded altogether the eligibility of twenty-two other countries. Chile was the only country to qualify continuously. As the data used by these authors would have been readily available to market participants, deterioration in those data, foretelling a loss of eligibility, would be a very serious matter; it could itself expose a country to a severe crisis. Transparency is desirable, but too much transparency may generate vulnerability.

It should be acknowledged, of course, that the risk of giving adverse signals to market participants may be offset by the incentive effects of participation in the proposed facility. It could perhaps encourage countries to manage their debts and fiscal policies more effectively in order to gain and retain their access to it. There is no way of knowing, however, which effect will dominate. The risk of an adverse market reaction might be minimized, however, if decisions about eligibility or its termination were based on the Fund's regular surveillance of a country's economy. This might be done before the

---

[28] Tito Cordella and Eduardo Levy Yeyati, "A (New) Country Insurance Facility," *International Finance* 9 (2006), pp. 1–36.

release of the surveillance report, depriving market participants in advance of any simple way to identify countries susceptible to termination.

IMF LENDING INTO ARREARS

At present, the IMF will not discontinue its lending when a member country fails to meet its obligations to its foreign creditors, provided the country is "dealing in good faith with its foreign creditors." In the Argentine case, however, the Fund continued to lend even when it was manifestly clear that Argentina was not consulting closely with its creditors and, in the end, Argentina made a take-it-or-leave-it offer to those creditors, an offer that imposed huge losses. This episode raises two questions, and the managing director tried to address them: One, should the Fund express views on the macroeconomic parameters that condition a country's ability to service its debt, whether in whole or in part? And two, how can one decide operationally whether a country is making a good-faith effort to reach a debt settlement with its foreign creditors?

Addressing himself to the first question, the managing director noted that a country's ability to service its debt, in whole or in part, should be judged on the basis of "an agreed medium-term fiscal envelope and macroeconomic framework on which the Fund expresses a clear view," even if the country concerned does not have a Fund program. This premise is widely accepted, he adds, but was not applied in the Argentine case.[29]

Addressing himself to the second question, the managing director suggested that the Fund's policy of lending into arrears needs to be reconsidered. The policy was based initially on the "structured negotiating framework of the 1980s ... whereas the recent experience has consisted of consultations via financial advisors, consideration of secondary market prices, and debt exchange offers."[30] This can perhaps be taken to mean that the Fund should play a larger role in sovereign debt negotiations, as indeed it did in the 1980s, or move to the opposite extreme and decline to lend into arrears. But the

---

[29] William R. Cline takes the same view; see Truman, ed., *Reforming the IMF,* p. 312.
[30] *Managing Director's Report,* p. 8.

26

managing director declined to pose that choice so starkly. In my view, the Fund should play a larger role, although the managing director has rightly noted that today's debt problems are different from those of the 1980s. The Fund should be prepared to translate its estimate of the debtor's "fiscal envelope and macroeconomic framework" into an estimate of the debtor's capacity to repay its creditors, and if the debtor refuses to offer its creditors repayment roughly commensurate with the Fund's estimate, the Fund should cease lending into arrears.

CHOOSING THE FUND'S MANAGING DIRECTOR

Throughout the history of the Fund, its managing director has been a European, and there has been just one instance in which the United States had reservations about the Europeans' choice. In that case, the United States agreed to accept him if he had widespread support, but its reservations diluted support for the candidate, and he was not chosen.[31] As part of the same tacit transatlantic bargain, the United States has enjoyed the right to choose the president of the World Bank, as well as the first deputy managing director of the IMF.

These arrangements are obsolete and should be replaced quickly, and the managing director has included this issue in his reform agenda. The Fund's members, he says, should respond by adopting and publishing guidelines for the selection of the managing director. There is, however, a case for going further. The secretary-general of the United Nations is nominated by the UN Security Council and then elected formally by the UN General Assembly. An analogous procedure could and should be adopted by the IMF and the World Bank.

The Fund's executive board should be charged with producing a short list of candidates (and should not be prevented from including one of the Fund's principal officials or, for that matter, a member of the existing executive board). The list of candidates should then be submitted to the Fund's governing board at its annual meeting,

---

[31] On this and other episodes involving the choice of the managing director, see Miles Kahler, *Leadership Selection in the Major Multilaterals* (Washington, DC: Institute for International Economics, 2001).

and the successful candidate should be the one who commands the support of a weighted majority of the Fund's membership—those casting no less than 70 percent of the quota-based votes. Alternatively, election of the managing director could require a double majority: a 70 percent majority of the quota-based votes plus a 70 percent majority of the Fund's membership, with each member having a single vote.[32]

Most of the Fund's managing directors have been effective leaders of the institution. But equally effective leaders could come from other countries, including some of the emerging-market countries. An open and transparent choice of the managing director would surely enhance the legitimacy of the Fund and banish the widespread belief that the Fund is run by and for the major industrial countries.

A NOTE ON MORE RADICAL REFORMS

Although the set of reforms proposed by the managing director would greatly improve the functioning of the Fund, some recent critics have called for more radical changes in the Fund's governance. One such suggestion is appealing, but on close inspection, rather unworkable. It has been suggested that the executive board be composed of highly qualified individuals rather than the representatives of national governments. In effect, the board would function much like the monetary policy committee of an independent central bank, with each member having just one vote.[33] They could be appointed by national governments or groups of governments and would be accountable to the IMFC.

Proponents of this scheme, however, neglect two basic differences between the executive board of the Fund and the monetary policy committee of an independent central bank. The latter has a well-defined objective, typically the maintenance of price

---

[32] Similar proposals have been made for the conduct of business by the executive board but are open to a serious objection. Decisions by the board often involve financial commitments by the Fund, and the governments providing most of those resources would surely oppose a regime that gave a large number of rather small countries considerable influence over the use of those resources.

[33] José De Gregorio, Barry Eichengreen, Takatoshi Ito, and Charles Wyplosz, *An Independent and Accountable IMF* (Geneva: International Center for Monetary and Banking Studies, 1999); Guillermo Le Fort V, in Ariel Buira, ed., *Reforming the Governance of the IMF*.

stability. The board of the Fund, by contrast, has a multidimensional task, and its performance would be very hard to monitor. Furthermore, the executive directors of the Fund have a fiduciary responsibility for the funds contributed by the member governments of the IMF. It would then fall to the members of the IMFC, representing governments, to exercise far closer oversight of the executive board. The board could not be fully independent; it would instead function in the shadow of the IMFC, and professional expertise would not protect the members of the board from political pressures.

There are ways to improve the functioning of the executive board. Thus, staggered elections for longer terms could provide more continuity in decision-making, and greater openness by management itself, including a willingness to inform the board of disagreements among the staff, would do a great deal to improve decision-making by the board.

CONCLUSION

The Fund's reform agenda is not yet complete, and the usefulness of some reforms, such as multilateral surveillance and a new precautionary facility, cannot be judged in advance. But both the world and the United States need a more effective Fund, and the effectiveness of the Fund depends importantly on its perceived legitimacy. Although this Special Report has expressed reservations about some of the managing director's proposals and has suggested modifications, his initiative is surely to be welcomed and fully deserves the support of the United States. A larger role for the developing countries—a key objective of the plan to overhaul the Fund—will not impair the influence of the United States. Rather, it will enhance that influence insofar as it increases the effectiveness of the IMF and enhances the Fund's role in the stabilization of the world economy and the resolution of disputes like those that have arisen from global imbalances.

It is important, moreover, that the United States do all it can to keep the reform process on track with a view to meeting the 2008 deadline for agreement on a new quota formula and the subsequent increase of quotas required for it to take effect. The issues are complex and controversial, and there is a significant risk of slippage. The apparent failure of the Doha Round of trade negotiations poses a threat to the multilateral system as a whole, and the resulting movement toward regional trading arrangements could well foster a trend to regional arrangements in the monetary sphere as well. To head off this fragmentation of the multilateral system, Congress should play its role responsibly. When asked to approve quota reform and other improvements to the IMF's governance, it must not drag its feet.

Moreover, it is essential to remember that the chief task of the Fund today is different from its task when it was established. The Bretton Woods Conference designed the IMF to govern a monetary system based on fixed exchange rates. Today, however, the Fund's primary task is crisis management, and it must be performed in close collaboration with the private sector. We may not see any looming crisis now, but economic and financial conditions can change with alarming speed, and crises are bound to recur. We will then look to the Fund to deal with them, and it must be equipped with the financial and human resources required to do that successfully.

REFERENCES

Bini Smaghi, Lorenzo. "A Single EU Seat in the IMF?" *Journal of Common Market Studies* 42 (June 2004), pp. 229–48.

Bini Smaghi, Lorenzo. "IMF Governance and the Political Economy of a Consolidated European Seat," in Edwin M. Truman, ed., *Reforming the IMF for the 21st Century*. Washington, DC: Institute for International Economics, 2006, Ch. 10.

Bordo, Michael D. and Harold James. "The International Monetary Fund: Its Present Role in Historical Perspective." National Bureau of Economic Research Working Paper No. 7724 (June 2000).

Broz, J. Lawrence. "The Role of the United States Congress," in Ariel Buira, ed., *Reforming the Governance of the IMF and the World Bank*. London: Anthem Press, 2005, Ch. 12.

Buira, Ariel, ed., *Reforming the Governance of the IMF and the World Bank*. London: Anthem Press, 2005.

Buira, Ariel. "The Bretton Woods Institutions: Governance without Legitimacy," in Ariel Buira, ed., *Reforming the Governance of the IMF and the World Bank*. London: Anthem Press, 2005, Ch. 2.

Cline, William R. "The Case for a Lender-of-Last Resort Role for the IMF," in Edwin M. Truman, ed., *Reforming the IMF for the 21st Century*. Washington, DC: Institute for International Economics, 2006, Ch. 14.

Cordella, Tito, and Eduardo Levy Yeyati, "A (New) Country Insurance Facility," *International Finance* 9 (2006), pp. 1–36.

De Gregorio, José, et al., *An Independent and Accountable IMF: Geneva Reports on the World Economy* 1. London: Centre for Economic Policy Research, October 1999, available at http://www.cepr.org/pubs/books/P130.asp.

Derviş, Kemal, with Ceren Özer. *A Better Globalization: Legitimacy, Government, and Reform*. Washington, DC: Center for Global Development, 2005.

dos Reis, Laura. "Measuring Vulnerability: Capital Flows Volatility in the Quota Formula," in Ariel Buira, ed., *Reforming the Governance of the IMF and the World Bank*. London: Anthem Press, 2005, Ch. 8.

Henning, C. Randall. *The Exchange Stabilization Fund: Slush Money or War Chest*, Washington, DC: Institute for International Economics, May 1999.

International Monetary Fund. *Articles of Agreement*, Washington, DC: International Monetary Fund, 1993.

International Monetary Fund. *Quotas—Updated Calculations*, Washington, DC: International Monetary Fund, 2004.

International Monetary Fund. *The Managing Director's Report on Implementing the Fund's Medium-Term Strategy*, Washington, DC: International Monetary Fund, April 5, 2006.

International Monetary Fund. *The Fund's Income Position for FY 2007—Midyear Review*, Washington, DC: International Monetary Fund, December 7, 2006.

International Monetary Fund, *Final Report of the Committee to Study Sustainable Financing of the IMF*, Washington, DC: International Monetary Fund, January 31, 2007.

International Monetary Fund, *IMF's International Monetary and Financial Committee Reviews Multilateral Consultation*, IMF Press Release 07/02, Washington, DC: International Monetary Fund, April 14, 2007.

International Monetary Fund and World Bank. *Final Report of the External Review Committee on Bank-Fund Collaboration*. Washington, DC: International Monetary Fund and World Bank, February 2007.

International Monetary and Financial Committee of the Board of Governors of the International Monetary Fund, *Communiqué*, Washington, DC: International Monetary Fund, September 17, 2006.

Kahler, Miles. *Leadership Selection in the Major Multinationals*. Washington, DC: Institute for International Economics, 2001.

Kelkar, Vijay, et al. "Reforming the International Monetary Fund: Toward Enhanced Accountability and Legitimacy," in Ariel Buira, ed., *Reforming the Governance of the IMF and the World Bank*. London: Anthem Press, 2005, Ch. 3.

Kenen, Peter B. *Financing, Adjustment, and the International Monetary Fund*. Washington, DC: The Brookings Institution, 1986.

Lachman, Desmond. "How Should IMF Resources Be Expanded?" in Edwin N. Truman, ed., *Reforming the IMF for the 21st Century*. Washington, DC: Institute for International Economics, 2006, Ch. 23.

Lane, Timothy. "Tensions in the Role of the IMF and Directions for Reform," *World Economics* 6 (2005), pp. 47–66.

Le Fort V., Guillermo. "Issues on IMF Governance and Representation," in Ariel Buira, ed., *Reforming the Governance of the IMF and the World Bank*. London: Anthem Press, 2005, Ch. 5.

Lerrick, Adam. "Funding the IMF: How Much Does It Really Cost?" Pittsburgh: Carnegie Mellon University, *Galliot Center on Public Policy Quarterly International Economics Report*, November 2003.

Mahieu, Géraldine, Dirk Ooms, and Stéphanie Rotter. "The Governance of the International Monetary Fund with a Single EU Chair," National Bank of Belgium *Financial Stability Review* (June 2003), pp.173–88.

McLenaghan, John B. "Purchasing Power Parities and Comparisons of GDP in IMF Quota Calculations," in Ariel Buira, ed., *Reforming the Governance of the IMF and the World Bank*. London: Anthem Press, 2005, Ch. 7.

Meltzer, Allan H. "New Mandates for the IMF and World Bank," *Cato Journal* (Winter 2005), pp. 13–16.

Mirakor, Abbas, and Iqbal Zaidi. "Rethinking the Governance of the International Monetary Fund," IMF Working Paper WP/06/273. Washington, DC: International Monetary Fund, December 2006.

Mussa, Michael. "Reflections on the Function and Facilities for IMF Lending," in Edwin M. Truman, ed., *Reforming the IMF for the 21st Century*. Washington, DC: Institute for International Economics, 2006, Ch. 21.

Padoa-Schioppa, Tommaso, "The IMF in Perspective," in Edwin M. Truman, ed., *Reforming the IMF for the 21st Century*. Washington, DC: Institute for International Economics, 2006, Ch. 27.

Truman, Edwin M., ed. *Reforming the IMF for the 21st Century*. Washington, DC: Institute for International Economics, 2006.

Van Houtven, Leo. *Governance of the IMF*. Washington, DC: International Monetary Fund, Pamphlet Series No. 53, August 2002, available at http://www.imf.org/external/pubs/ft/pam/pam53/contents.html.

Woods, Ngaire. "Making the IMF and the World Bank More Accountable," in Ariel Buira, ed., *Reforming the Governance of the IMF and the World Bank*. London: Anthem Press, 2005, Ch.6.

APPENDIX A

Consolidating EU Representation				Other Countries' Constituencies		
EU Countries' Constituencies						
	Votes	**Countries**			**Votes**	**Countries**
Germany	130332	1		Antigua and Barbuda, etc:		
				Omit Ireland		
France	107635	1		**Modified Total**	**72002**	**11**
United Kingdom	107635	1		Denmark, etc:		
				Omit separate constituency.		
Austria	18973			moving Ireland and Norway to		
Belgium	46302			next constituency	---	---
Bulgaria	6652					
Czech Republic	8443			Costa Rica etc:		
Hungary	10634			Omit Spain		
Luxembourg	3041			Add:		
Poland	13940			Iceland	1426	
Romania	10552			Israel	9532	
Slovak Republic	3825			Norway	16967	
Slovenia	2567			San Marino	420	
				Timor-Leste	332	
Total	**124929**	**10**		**Modified Total**	**90927**	**12**
Denmark	16678			Azerbaijan, etc:		
Estonia	902			Omit Poland		
Finland	12888			Add:		
Ireland	8634			Albania	737	
Latvia	1518			Armenia	1170	
Lithuania	1692			Belarus	4.114	
Netherlands	51874			Bosnia & Herzegovina	1.941	
Sweden	24205			Croatia	1646	
				Georgia	1753	
Total	**118391**	**8**		Macedonia	939	
				Moldova	1484	
Cyprus	1646			Ukraine	13970	
Greece	8480			**Modified Total**	**75639**	**14**
Italy	70805					
Malta	1270					
Portugal	8924					
Spain	30739					
Total	**121864**	**6**				

36

ABOUT THE AUTHOR

Peter B. Kenen is a senior fellow in international economics at the Council on Foreign Relations and Walker Professor of Economics and International Finance Emeritus at Princeton University. He taught at Columbia University from 1957 to 1971, and then moved to Princeton, where he taught in the economics department and the Woodrow Wilson School and served for many years as director of the International Finance Section. He has written or coauthored several books, including *Asset Markets, Exchange Rates, and Economic Integration; Managing Exchange Rates;* and *Economic and Monetary Union in Europe.* He has published papers in many professional journals and edited several books, including *Managing the World Economy* and *Understanding Interdependence.* He has served as a consultant to the Council of Economic Advisers, the U.S. Treasury, and the Federal Reserve, as well as the International Monetary Fund. He was a member of President John F. Kennedy's Task Force on Foreign Economic Policy and the Economic Advisory Panel of the Federal Reserve Bank of New York. He has held research fellowships at the Center for Advanced Study in the Behavioral Sciences, the Royal Institute of International Affairs, the Bank of England, and other institutions. He is currently completing a book titled *Regional Monetary Integration.*

ADVISORY COMMITTEE FOR

REFORM OF THE INTERNATIONAL MONETARY FUND

Caroline Atkinson
COUNCIL ON FOREIGN RELATIONS

Nancy Birdsall
CENTER FOR GLOBAL DEVELOPMENT

James Boughton
INTERNATIONAL MONETARY FUND

Elaine Buckberg
NERA ECONOMIC CONSULTING

Andrew Crockett
J.P. MORGAN CHASE & CO.

Kristin J. Forbes
MASSACHUSETTS INSTITUTE OF
TECHNOLOGY

David D. Hale
HALE ADVISORS

Douglas Holtz-Eakin
JOHN MCCAIN 2008 EXPLORATORY
COMMITTEE

Yves-Andre Istel
ROTHSCHILD NORTH AMERICA, INC.

Brad W. Setser
ROUBINI GLOBAL ECONOMICS, INC.

Jeffrey R. Shafer
CITIGROUP GLOBAL MARKETS INC.

Amity R. Shlaes
COUNCIL ON FOREIGN RELATIONS

Kathleen Stephansen
CREDIT SUISSE

Daniel K. Tarullo
GEORGETOWN UNIVERSITY LAW
CENTER

Edwin M. Truman
INSTITUTE FOR INTERNATIONAL
ECONOMICS

Christine I. Wallich
THE WORLD BANK

Note: Council Special Reports reflect the judgments and recommendations of the author(s). They do not necessarily represent the views of members of the advisory committee, whose involvement in no way should be interpreted as an endorsement of the report by either themselves or the organizations with which they are affiliated.

COUNCIL SPECIAL REPORTS
SPONSORED BY THE COUNCIL ON FOREIGN RELATIONS

Nuclear Energy: Balancing Benefits and Risks
Charles D. Ferguson; CSR No. 28, April 2007

Nigeria: Elections and Continuing Challenges
Robert I. Rotberg; CSR No. 27, April 2007
A Center for Preventive Action Report

The Economic Logic of Illegal Immigration
Gordon H. Hanson; CSR No. 26, April 2007
A Maurice R. Greenberg Center for Geoeconomic Studies Report

The United States and the WTO Dispute Settlement System
Robert Z. Lawrence; CSR No. 25, March 2007
A Maurice R. Greenberg Center for Geoeconomic Studies Report

Bolivia on the Brink
Eduardo A. Gamarra; CSR No. 24, February 2007
A Center for Preventive Action Report

After the Surge: The Case for U.S. Military Disengagement from Iraq
Steven N. Simon; CSR No. 23, February 2007

Darfur and Beyond: What Is Needed to Prevent Mass Atrocities
Lee Feinstein; CSR No. 22, January 2007

Avoiding Conflict in the Horn of Africa: U.S. Policy Toward Ethiopia and Eritrea
Terrence Lyons; CSR No. 21, December 2006
A Center for Preventive Action Report

Living with Hugo: U.S. Policy Toward Hugo Chávez's Venezuela
Richard Lapper; CSR No. 20, November 2006
A Center for Preventive Action Report

Reforming U.S. Patent Policy: Getting the Incentives Right
Keith E. Maskus; CSR No. 19, November 2006
A Maurice R. Greenberg Center for Geoeconomic Studies Report

Foreign Investment and National Security: Getting the Balance Right
Alan P. Larson, David M. Marchick; CSR No. 18, July 2006
A Maurice R. Greenberg Center for Geoeconomic Studies Report

Challenges for a Postelection Mexico: Issues for U.S. Policy
Pamela K. Starr; CSR No. 17, June 2006 (web-only release) and November 2006

U.S.-India Nuclear Cooperation: A Strategy for Moving Forward
Michael A. Levi and Charles D. Ferguson; CSR No. 16, June 2006

Generating Momentum for a New Era in U.S.-Turkey Relations
Steven A. Cook and Elizabeth Sherwood-Randall; CSR No. 15, June 2006

Peace in Papua: Widening a Window of Opportunity
Blair A. King; CSR No. 14, March 2006
A Center for Preventive Action Report

Neglected Defense: Mobilizing the Private Sector to Support Homeland Security
Stephen E. Flynn and Daniel B. Prieto; CSR No. 13, March 2006

Afghanistan's Uncertain Transition From Turmoil to Normalcy
Barnett R. Rubin; CSR No. 12, March 2006
A Center for Preventive Action Report

Preventing Catastrophic Nuclear Terrorism
Charles D. Ferguson; CSR No. 11, March 2006

Getting Serious About the Twin Deficits
Menzie D. Chinn; CSR No. 10, September 2005
A Maurice R. Greenberg Center for Geoeconomic Studies Report

Both Sides of the Aisle: A Call for Bipartisan Foreign Policy
Nancy E. Roman; CSR No. 9, September 2005

Forgotten Intervention? What the United States Needs to Do in the Western Balkans
Amelia Branczik and William L. Nash; CSR No. 8, June 2005
A Center for Preventive Action Report

A New Beginning: Strategies for a More Fruitful Dialogue with the Muslim World
Craig Charney and Nicole Yakatan; CSR No. 7, May 2005

Power-Sharing in Iraq
David L. Phillips; CSR No. 6, April 2005
A Center for Preventive Action Report

Giving Meaning to "Never Again": Seeking an Effective Response to the Crisis in Darfur and Beyond
Cheryl O. Igiri and Princeton N. Lyman; CSR No. 5, September 2004

Freedom, Prosperity, and Security: The G8 Partnership with Africa: Sea Island 2004 and Beyond
J. Brian Atwood, Robert S. Browne, and Princeton N. Lyman; CSR No. 4, May 2004

Addressing the HIV/AIDS Pandemic: A U.S. Global AIDS Strategy for the Long Term
Daniel M. Fox and Princeton N. Lyman; CSR No. 3, May 2004
Cosponsored with the Milbank Memorial Fund

Challenges for a Post-Election Philippines
Catharin E. Dalpino; CSR No. 2, May 2004
A Center for Preventive Action Report

Stability, Security, and Sovereignty in the Republic of Georgia
David L. Phillips; CSR No. 1, January 2004
A Center for Preventive Action Report

To purchase a printed copy, call the Brookings Institution Press: 800-537-5487.
Note: Council Special Reports are available to download from the Council's website, CFR.org.
For more information, contact publications@cfr.org.